Lake Huron

Great Lakes of North America

Harry Beckett

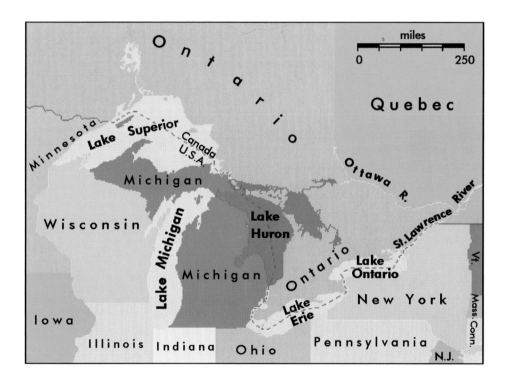

The Rourke Corporation, Inc.
Vero Beach, Florida 32964

PHOTO CREDITS:
Photographs by kind permission of: Wasaga Beach Provincial Park; Huronia Museum, Midland, Ontario; Archives of Ontario; Port Huron Museum, Port Huron, Michigan; Mackinac Island State Park; Geovisuals, Waterloo, Ontario; Fathom National Marine Park, Tobermory, Ontario; Collingwood Museum, Collingwood, Ontario; Jack Poste; Maps by J. David Knox

CREATIVE SERVICES:
East Coast Studios, Merritt Island, Florida

EDITORIAL SERVICES:
Susan Albury

Library of Congress Cataloging-in-Publication Data

Beckett, Harry, 1936-
    Lake Huron / by Harry Beckett.
        p. cm. — (Great Lakes of North America)
    Includes bibliographical references and index.
    Summary: Discusses Lake Huron's geography, history, early inhabitants, important events, economy, and more.
        ISBN 0-86593-525-4
    1. Huron, Lake (Mich. and Ont.) Juvenile literature. [1. Huron, Lake (Mich. and Ont.)] I. Title. II. Series: Beckett, Harry, 1936- Great Lakes of North America.
F554.B43 1999
977.4—dc21
                                                    99-13024
                                                    CIP

Printed in the USA

TABLE OF CONTENTS

FACTS AND FIGURES FOR LAKE HURON

Length	206 miles	332 kilometers
Width	183 miles	294 kilometers
Average depth	195 feet	59 meters
Maximum depth	750 feet	229 meters
Volume	850 cubic miles	3,540 cubic kilometers
Water surface area	23,000 sq. miles	59,600 sq. kilometers
Shoreline (inc. islands)	3,827 miles	6,157 kilometers
Area of basin	51,700 sq. miles	134,100 sq. kilometers
Height above sea level	577 feet	176 meters
Retention time*	22 years	

* The average time that it takes for a molecule of water to enter and leave the lake

4

ABOUT LAKE HURON

In area, Lake Huron is the second largest of the Great Lakes, and the fifth largest lake in the world. The Province of Ontario lies to its north, east, and south, and the state of Michigan to its west. Sixty percent of the lake lies in Canada and forty percent in the United States.

Georgian Bay, its northeastern arm, is often called the sixth Great Lake because it is divided from the main body of Lake Huron by the Bruce Peninsula and Manitoulin Island. Alone, it would be among the twenty largest lakes in the world. The Lower Michigan Peninsula is called the Michigan Mitt because it looks like a mitten, with Saginaw Bay cutting off the thumb from the palm of the hand.

Lake Huron receives its water from Lake Superior through the Saint Mary's River, from Lake Michigan through the Straits of Mackinac, and from many feeder rivers. The French and Severn Rivers (Ontario) and the Au Sable River (Michigan) were all important in the early exploration and development of the Great Lakes. Water leaves Huron through the Saint Clair River.

Summer fun along Lake Huron's shore

The northern and eastern shores are rugged Canadian Shield, with many bays and inlets. A rocky limestone **escarpment** (eh SKARP munt) runs northward from Niagara Falls, up the Bruce Peninsula, across Manitoulin, and through the islands parallel to the northern shore.

Southern Georgian Bay and the eastern and western shores of Lake Huron have sandy beaches and high sand dunes, formed by the action of water and wind. The Michigan shore is called the sunrise side, and the Ontario shore is famous for its spectacular sunsets.

Swamps, marshes, bogs, and fens, called wetlands, form in areas around the lake, where the water table comes up to or near the land surface. They provide a **habitat** (HAB uh tat) for aquatic life, prevent erosion, and control pollution.

NATIVE PEOPLES AND EARLY EXPLORERS

The Native peoples of the Great Lakes lived by hunting, gathering, farming, and fishing, and often **migrated** (MY gray tid) from region to region. Sometimes they were looking for new hunting grounds; sometimes their land became infertile; sometimes stronger forces pushed them out.

When Europeans first appeared on Lake Huron, the Huron, or Wyandot, were living a settled, farming life on southeastern Georgian Bay. Traveling in their light birchbark canoes, they traded as far away as Quebec City, the Carolinas, and the **subarctic** (sub ARK tik).

The Ottawa (their own word for trader) on Manitoulin Island and in northern Michigan were go-betweens in east-west trade. With the Potawatami of southern Michigan and the Ojibwa of northern Michigan, they made up the Confederacy of the Three Fires.

The Menominee harvested wild rice in the wetlands, and the Potawatami even fished at night by the light of fires on the prows of their boats.

The Huron were a confederacy of four nations (Bear, Cord, Rock, and Deer), each with eight clans. This warrior is from the Turtle Clan.

Numbering of the Indians at Wequamikoong, Lake Huron, by Capt. Ironsides, Indian Supt, and Francis Assikinack, chief of 24 tribes, Aug. 16, 1856. Note the European influences.

The first European explorer on Lake Huron was probably Étienne Brulé. Samuel de Champlain sent him to live among the Huron in 1610. Later, he reached the Saint Mary's River, the entrance to Lake Superior. We know little about Brulé or his wide travels.

Champlain, however, made maps, sketches, and records on his own travels. He entered the lake through the Ottawa River system and spent the winter of 1614 and 1615 among the Huron, becoming their trading partner. He was sorry that they did not accept Christianity with enthusiasm, but he admired their way of life.

The French established a mission at Sault Sainte Marie among the Huron. Friendship with the French hurt the Huron. The French were fighting with the British over the fur trade. In 1648, the Iroquois, allies of the British, began fierce attacks on the Huron, killing many. Also, as many as two thirds died of European diseases. By 1652, the remaining Huron had moved to Quebec or to a Wyandot reservation in Oklahoma. The Iroquois even adopted some. This is called the **dispersal** (duh SPUR sul) of the Huron. During the Iroquois wars, five Jesuit priests were martyred, including Jean de Brébeuf, who later became a saint.

Louis Jolliet, a French trapper, canoed down Lake Huron in 1669 to discover Lake Erie. The first white settler, a French fur trader called Louis Chevelier, arrived in the Tawas area only in 1800.

A meeting between a Potawatami, missionaries, and traders before the building of Fort St. Joseph in 1686. Fort St. Joseph is located near Port Huron.

TOWNS AND CITIES

The Lake Huron shoreline is sparsely populated. Sarnia (Ontario) and Port Huron (Michigan), its two largest cities, lie side by side at the southern end of the lake. They are separated only by the Saint Clair River, and connected to each other by a rail tunnel under the river and the Blue Water Bridge over it.

Sarnia (population 74,164) is one of Ontario's busiest ports and boating centers. The new Centre by the Bay houses a science center with exhibits and **interactive** (in tuh RAK tiv) displays. Under the Blue Water Bridge, a working model of the Great Lakes explains their ecology, water cycles, history, and geography.

15

Port Huron (population 33,362) is a major deepwater port. Thomas Alva Edison, the U.S. inventor, lived there from the ages of 7 to 16. He had only three months of formal schooling—his mother taught him at home. But he had a laboratory in his basement and it was in Port Huron that he learned and developed many new telegraphic techniques. The Port Huron to Mackinac Island Race is the world's largest freshwater sailing event. The city was also a major station on the **Underground Railroad** (UN dur graund RAYL rode).

Bay City has over 250 structures on the National Historic Register, many dating from its days as the "lumber capital of the world." Saginaw Bay has been widened and deepened to accommodate the lakes' largest ships.

Alpena, Tawas, and Harbor Beach on the Michigan shore and Goderich, Owen Sound, and Parry Sound in Ontario are small ports that serve their surrounding area.

A statue of Thomas A. Edison. In the background, a second span to the Blue Water Bridge is under construction.

Collingwood was once called Hen and Chickens. It lies on Georgian Bay at the northern end of the shortest land route between the upper and lower lakes, and once hoped to be the major city that Chicago became.

The rocky and wooded northern shore of Lake Huron is dotted with small, isolated communities that are dependent upon lumber and mineral industries. Until the mid-1950s they had no road or railroad to serve them.

Owen Sound. A sound is a sheltered inlet.

WORKING AROUND THE LAKE

The Lake Huron area was once covered with forests that gave the aboriginal peoples food, clothing, shelter, and fuel. To the first Europeans the forests meant furs and farmland where they could clear the trees. In the eighteenth century, lumber built the navies of the nations fighting to control the Great Lakes. Now, the forests supply the pulp and paper mills and sawmills. Towns such as Tawas on the Au Sable River and Goderich, Ontario, which was only opened up around 1820, were founded on lumbering, hunting, and fishing. Bay City once built the world's largest sailing ships. Earlier this century, it produced ready-built wooden houses to be sold through major catalogs.

Now tourists come to the forests, rivers, and sandy beaches for hunting, fishing, and boating, or skiing and snowmobiling in winter. Fathom Five National Park at Tobermory, on the rocky Bruce Peninsula, is famous for its shoreline and underwater beauty.

Most industry is in the south. The first **commercial** (kuh MUR shul) oil well in North America was drilled at Sarnia. It has a busy chemical and petroleum industry. Port Huron has close connections to the industrial centers of Detroit, Flint, and Lansing. Over three million vehicles a year pass between the United States and Canada across the Blue Water Bridge.

The nuclear plant at Douglas Point on Bruce Peninsula provides jobs and power.

Agriculture on the eastern shore is mostly mixed farming. The top of the Michigan mitt has areas of sandy soil and enough moisture to grow grains and potatoes. Early German and Dutch settlers brought farming to the thumb. It has a longer growing season and produces beets, beans, potatoes, and fruit.

The rocky Bruce Peninsula

But, above all, Lake Huron is part of the Saint Lawrence Waterway and shipping is the major industry. Long, narrow ships called lakers carry iron ore to Lake Erie ports or grain from the prairies. More tons of shipping pass under the Blue Water Bridge in one season than pass through the Suez and Panama Canals combined.

Oil storage tanks at Sarnia. Tankers carry oil to ports all around the Great Lakes.

DISASTERS AND MYSTERIES

Lake Huron's worst storm began to form on November 6, 1913. During its fiercest 16 hours, winds averaged 60 miles per hour (96 kilometers per hour). They piled up waves 35 feet (10.7 meters) high and so close together that it caused ten ships, eight of them Great Lakes freighters, to **founder** (FOUN der). Twenty-five other vessels ran aground, many becoming total wrecks. Two hundred and forty-eight sailors lost their lives. Two freighters, the *Matoa* and the *Howard M. Hanna* sank in Saginaw Bay. The *James C. Carruthers*, which sank in southern Lake Huron, was the largest ship on the lakes at the time and only 172 days old.

The 1913 storm gave rise to one of the Great Lakes' mysteries. The freighter *Charles S. Price*, new, well-equipped, and fully loaded with coal, was lost with all its crew. Some of its crew were found later, drowned, but wearing lifebelts from the freighter *Regina*, which sank fifteen miles away. The storm raged for five days.

The explorer René-Robert Cavelier de La Salle built the *Griffon*, the first commercial craft to sail the lakes above Niagara Falls, in 1679. It was launched on the Niagara River and set sail along Lake Erie, through the Detroit and Saint Claire Rivers into Lake Huron, north through stormy weather to Fort Michilimackinac, and on to Green Bay on Lake Michigan. On September 18, the *Griffon* sailed off on its return journey, carrying La Salle's fortune in beaver pelts, leaving La Salle behind to continue his explorations. The Griffon, with its crew of five commanded by the pilot, Lucas, said to be seven foot tall, disappeared into history.

A model of the Griffon, *on a scale of 1/4 inch to 1 foot*

At least two wrecks in Lake Huron could be the *Griffon*. One was on the rocky western tip of Manitoulin Island. Six skeletons were found near this site, one of them of great size. The other wreck was on Russell Island, off the Bruce Peninsula. This ship could have been of the same size and date as the *Griffon*. Did the crew, angry at not being paid, beach the ship and steal the cargo? Did a terrible storm wreck it? Or was it seized by Indians? After three hundred years, the *Griffon*'s fate is still a mystery.

A painting of the burning of the Manitoulin, *done in 1882 by a child who witnessed the event.*

INTERESTING PLACES

The aboriginal peoples thought an island at the entrance to the Straits of Mackinac looked like a turtle and gave it the name Michilimackinac (mich-la-MACK-in-aw). We call it Mackinac Island (MACK-in-aw).

Jean Nicolet was probably the first European to see the island in 1634, after he crossed Lake Huron with seven Huron braves. It became a French fur-trading station. When the British won control of the straits in 1780, they built a fort on the island. The United States held it for a time.

In 1812, fast canoes from the lower lakes brought news to the British that they were at war with the United States. They took the U.S. garrison by surprise and seized the fort. Finally, a **treaty** (TREE tee) gave it back to the United States.

Mackinac Island became the center of John Jacob Astor's American Fur Company. When the fur trade and commercial fishing **declined** (dee KLIND), tourists flocked to the island to enjoy the sportfishing and to build vacation homes. The island has a nature center, parkland, bicycle and hiking trails, car-free streets, and some of Michigan's oldest buildings. Costumed interpreters show what life was like at Fort Mackinac, and visitors can learn to load and fire muskets and cannons.

The Nancy Island Ontario Provincial Park is at Wasaga Beach on Georgian Bay. After the Battle of Put-in-Bay on Lake Erie, the United States cut off British supply routes to the upper lakes. The British had to send their supplies by land and water to the mouth of the Nottawasaga River. From there, H.M.S. *Nancy*, the only British ship left on the upper lakes, transported them to Mackinac Island. In 1814, three U.S. ships caught the *Nancy* in the Nottawasaga and sank her. Her commander, Lieutenant Worsley with his crew, twenty natives and eight voyageurs rowed 360 miles (580 kilometers) to Fort Mackinac.

A U.S. soldier on guard at Fort Mackinac, a National Park since 1875

There, he seized two of the U.S. ships, the *Tigress* and the *Scorpion*, and regained control of the supply route until the war ended, one year later.

Sand and silt formed an island around the wreck of the *Nancy*. The hull, recovered in 1928, is now in a museum on the island. The river, once the home of aboriginal peoples and later a lumber community, is now lined by modern homes and cottages.

Wasaga Beach, the world's longest freshwater beach. The Nottawasaga River and Mancy Island in the background.

GLOSSARY

commercial (kuh MUR shul) — having to do with business

decline (dee KLINE) — to become less or weaker

dispersal (duh SPUR sul) — a scattering in different directions

escarpment (eh SKARP munt) — a steep fall or drop, such as a line of cliffs

founder (FOUN der) — to sink after filling up with water

habitat (HAB uh tat) — the kind of place where an animal or plant usually lives

interactive (in tuh RAK tiv) — that in which the viewer participates

migrate (MY grayt) — to move from one living place to another

subarctic (sub ARK tik) — the region surrounding the Arctic Circle

treaty (TREE tee) — a formal agreement between states

underground railroad (UN dur graund RAYL rode) — a system which, before 1861, helped escaped slaves to reach Canada or the free states

INDEX

FURTHER READING

You can find out more about the Great Lakes with these helpful books and web sites:
- Pierre Berton. *The Great Lakes,* Stoddart
- *Alone In The Night*, Lynx Images: www.lynximages.com
- F. Stonehouse. *Went Missing,* Avery Color Studios
- R.J. Hemming. *Ships Gone Missing*

- Great Lakes Information Network: www.great-lakes.net
- Environmental Protection Agency: www.epa.gov/glnpo
- Sea Grant Program: www.d.umn.edu/seagr/gallery.html
- Tourism and history: www.cglg.org/projects/tourism & http://www.gov.on.ca
- Native peoples: www.dickshovel.com & www.schoolnet.ca
- A Quiz on the Lakes: www.hebe.edu.on.ca/coll/lakes.htm